TIME BOMB

TIME BOMB

Poems

Richard H. Fox

KITTACUCK PRESS
Worcester, Massachusetts

Designed and composed in Kepler Std and Cronos Pro at Hobblebush Books, Brookline, NH (www.hobblebush.com).

Printed in the United States of America

Front cover photograph:
On the Roof by Mark William Rabiner: gallery.leica-users.org/v/lugalrabs

Back cover photograph:
Dan Tappan, dantappanphotos.com

Page 18 photograph:
Charis Wilson, 1935. Photograph by Edward Weston. Collection Center for Creative Photography, © 1981 Center for Creative Photography, Arizona Board of Regents

ISBN: 978-0-9893127-0-7

Library of Congress Control Number: 2013910932

Published by:

KITTACUCK PRESS
6 Jamesburg Drive,
Worcester, Massachusetts 01609

www.kittacuck.com

For Ann, Dan, & Adam
Mom & Dad
thank you for my life

Contents

Rue

Better living through cancer

Clan Webster

Keeping time for my history

Acknowledgments

Grateful acknowledgment is made to the following publications in which these poems first appeared or are forthcoming, some in an earlier form:

About Place Journal: "CAT Scan"

The Apeiron Review: "1971"

Boston Literary Magazine: "Dad says Grace" and "Mrs. Noah's Bitch"

Camroc Press Review: "Chemo Brain" and "A recent National Geographic
    survey indicates that eleven per cent of the young people in this country
    can't locate the United States on a map"

Concrete Wolf: "In the Nick of Time"

Fat City Review: "Anesthesia" and "Sound and Sense"

Maelstrom: "Oh, Missouri"

Midstream Magazine: "TUNIS"

OVS: "Moses on The Green Line"

Poetry Quarterly: "Taxi Dancer (July 1975)"

Sahara: "The Devil talks to his teenage son and gets raked over the coals" and
    "The Fifth Floor"

Soul-Lit: "Agita," "John Lennon writes a note to Sean's teacher," and
    "Nitrous Oxide"

twist: "The antique store," "Niagara Falls, 1972," and "Rue"

The Worcester Review: "Joan Ellis, rest peacefully"

Appreciation to the following journals who republished poems, some in
an earlier form:

Ibbetson Street: "The Fifth Floor"

The Niagara Poetry Project: "Niagara Falls, 1972"

Sahara: "The antique store"

Soul-Lit: "The Fifth Floor" and "TUNIS"

Heartfelt thanks to John Hodgen for mentoring, editing, and delivering
this book.

    Mark William Rabiner, thanks for the cover image and for inspiring me
with your vision and insight.

    Appreciation for Judy Ferrara and Dan Lewis for their invaluable advice
and Kristina England for suggesting the book's title.

    I'm grateful for my writing groups: Southgate Workshop and Poetry
Happens Workshop. My poems come of age in villages.

    Thanks to BeJae Fleming for encouragement, support, and friendship.

    Stanley Kunitz was asked why this old mill town breeds so many poets. His
response: *People in Worcester are provoked to poetry!* I second that motion.

Rue

There's man all over for you, blaming on
his boots the fault of his feet.

SAMUEL BECKETT
WAITING FOR GODOT, 1954

John Lennon writes a note to Sean's teacher

Dear Ms. Goodenberry,

Sean was absent from school yesterday
I might say he was ill but that'd be a lie
We kept him home because he was well   naked
and lying on an empty canvas in Yoko's studio
he dipped his palms in paint   spun in
circles   ovals   diamonds
using elbows knees forehead backside
even his penis to draw daydreams
by the time he was bored it was too late to
          get the paint washed off

I once got in trouble in Art School for coming
into class with oils and charcoal all over my kit
didn't want Sean to go through the same grief
nor you because you are a gentle soul
who follows the rules and tries to act stern
enclosed is a Polaroid of the canvas
far beyond a boy's homework assignment

Ta for now, peace and luv,
John

Rue

The barrel tastes a cross between anchovies and eggplant,
warm after entering my mouth. I lie here in a red teddy,
eyes closed, a half naked mannequin. You are the only
one I trust to squeeze the trigger. What I see is a man
who weeps, imagine you the finger releasing
the safety. You saw me an oasis, filled your
stomach until you heaved sand. Sleep
will evade you for a year or two,
then the lines in your face
will fade. I am a cross
between sweetbreads
and sour cream.
Buy me this
last round
darling.

Moses on The Green Line

Riverside I close Zohar Manna's *Mathematical*
  Theory of Computation rub my eyes then temples.
A man in a shoulder to ankle white robe etched
  with sand cracked sandals dry toenails
  grasps a plastic loop. He sways with the car
  hums a tune in minor key to the rhythm of the rail.

I catch his eyes and He winks lined face
  lesions cover upper cheeks long beard pure
  white whiter than his robe.
He glances down at my book asks "Food for thought?"
"Debugging, fixpoints, and flowcharts." I answer
"Debugging?" He repeats and giggles "Language is a
  mangled art. Only babel is clear."

At the Reservoir stop He waves his arms.
  The seat next to me opens. He sits
  robe pooling against my bare legs
  gestures to the roof with his right hand
  burns on fingers burn on tongue when He speaks.
"I spent forty years wandering. But I knew
  where I was headed. Now you wander
  to find where to wander. Fixpoint."

He pops a Milk Dud in his mouth offers me one.
I nod no and answer "But when you could see
  The Promised Land, you were made an exile."
He holds his finger up finishes chewing
  "I had a job to do. Be the leader, the prophet,
  the teacher. And I learned how to chisel stone."

He shrugs a box of Raisinettes at my mouth.
  I look at him. He sighs continues.
"Look, I knew from the wicker basket my boss is tough.
  Ever think about wicker and wicked? Now wicked is
  good. Maybe it was then. Wicked awesome drown
  proof basket. Listen, do you think I liked the plagues?
  The tenth one wiped out most of my soccer side.

And my rod, cut from bamboo I cultivated and
harvested, turned into a snake when I was ordered
to throw it at Pharaoh's feet. For forty years,
I cut olive branches. You think they help marching?"

He reaches down and pulls up a box of Jordan Almonds
shakes it and chuckles "good and plenty good and
plenty. Just like Charlie on the choo-choo!"
I accept a handful pop one in my mouth the flavor
wanders it's like a fresh fallen twig soaked
in my saliva and woody can't remember an
older taste it dissolves and the subway car
appears.

He puts a hand over my eyes on top of my head hums
stashes a Heavenly Hash in my pocket
"This lesson, not entering The Promised Land,
is that the journey, not the endpoint, is life.
My climb down the mountain, tablets to breast.
My brother's golden calf. These weigh not on a
scale but on faith. This subway car, will you
remember the ride or that we stop at Fenway?"

On his head a kelly green cap with a big red B.
He tosses me a bag of fresh roasted peanuts,
waves his arms and exits the car.

Fun with Dick and Jane

Dick and Jane walk from the river
hand cold as spring water in hand damp as dew
bare soles burn over sunned rocks
they hop over gravel to grass   fall into a patch of shade

fingers draw lines and circles on her cheeks
a hand strokes his hair runs down his neck
Dick jams his lips against Jane's
braces bruise her mouth   she winces

he pulls away   clenches his teeth
leaping to his feet sparks burst in his eyes
the trees flicker as he gropes for an anchor
Dick's knees sink   Jane lifts under his arms

they hear his brother call from the parking lot
jump in the car as brother starts driving away
in the backseat curled against the door
brother's cigarette smoke passes over their heads

sun blinks between every tree and telephone pole
they sleep Jane's head on Dick's chest
he snores until a lit butt lands in his mouth
the car stops   he hollers at his brother's laughter

Jane slides out   trudges alone up her lawn
brother hisses *walk her to the door, dummy!*
Dick and Jane amble over a carpet of bluegrass
his shaking hand at the base of her spine

she leans into him   hand drops to brush his thigh
on the porch both start to speak   then giggle
he stutters bites a callous   she grins looks up
her hands on his hips   Jane grazes Dick's lips with hers

Brave

Hot springs, cold springs, the pond by Wachusett Cave.
Summer before senior year, boys and girls skinny bathe.
Sophomore Dara hitches a ride, promises to behave,
tells sister Sue she's old enough and in love with Dave.
Behind a pine tree, she disrobes, trying to be brave.
Naked but tunic, walks to water's edge, waves.
Sue glares in boys' eyes knowing what they crave.
Tunic torn from behind, boys toss it as they've
commenced a game of keep away in their enclave.
Dara covers up her breasts, sees who is depraved.
Laughing, cupping his chest, is Dave, mimicking a save.
She dives down, cheeks cherry red, voice a banshee rave.
Prick enslaved, her nails twist like a lathe, engrave.
Swallowing water, spitting, Dave's bawl is grave.

Sound and Sense

      Sandoval plucks his stubble
kneels to shuffle the bag of notions
Saffron's flea market discoveries
merchants frown at his hands gliding over shelves
fingertips skipping off this and that
but he never has broken one of their curios
Saffron's eyes are well versed in sifting
the vanilla from The Sandoval
      She sits at her secretary
purple pen shaping words on sky parchment
looks up after each line
is he signing or staring at the ceiling?
Sandoval's hands are covered with glue and solder
marrying sea glass to desert fossil
wrapping feathers around trip wire
when he spreads his arms to reach end to end
touching each element reviewing every bond
Saffron circles his biceps feeling him feel
her vision conjures titles for his sculptures
      When comfortable with a poem
she reads it to him in her curious accent
if sonant is indiscernible he taps her on the shoulder
Saffron fingers the letters into his palm
watches his lips form the word
once he commits stanzas to heart
she guides him to the dais under the window
Sandoval performs her poem
foot taps meter   arms oscillate
blood and burns on his skin lace delivery
she claps her hands until they are crimson
      They sup by scented candle
he spins vinyl von Schlippenbach Zorn Shipp
she views videos Buñuel Resnais Godard
sitting on the divan his head on her shoulder
he squeezes her hand when a solo levitates him
if she shudders he wipes her eyes laps his pads

In their bed Sandoval's fingers
tour Saffron   sinew seamount striation chasm
she sows her palms on his chest
rides each breath   howls at heartbeats
while they quake he trembles for her
while they quiver she ululates for him

The antique store

Angelina is the antique gliding between pine cabinets, the mouse who built her maze. She pulls her navy dress taut. One hand pinches the collar below her chin, the other shakes the ruffled waist. Arms linked, we face a mirror with teal flowers etched in its border. She angles my Tilley hat, evens the depressions above the brim. *My husband Theodore wore a Fedora. He passed last Fall. I miss fixing a man's hat.*

We edge by an 1875 casting couch, a radio that broadcast the attack on Pearl Harbor, around a bookcase filled with first editions of Nancy Drew and Tom Swift, to a mahogany chest. *These treasures are not for sale.* Her veined hands are steady as she winds key after key over a ring until finding the lock's mate. The ebony top is silent as it's raised. Angelina reaches in, cups a locket engraved "All my love, Ted, Sept 9 1935." She clicks the clasp revealing profiles of a youthful pair. The woman's eyes prance, lips pout. Dietrich must have been jealous. The man sports a thick mustache. *Theodore was a novelist, we traveled the world.* I tell Angelina I recognize her hat, that she is a beauty; she and the hat haven't lost style or charm. She pecks my cheek, moist. The wood ceiling fan raises my neck hair.

You'll enjoy this miniature. Angelina gingerly opens an oak frame inscribed "July 9 1865." It cracks as notches slide. She places the open frame under the locket. My eyes jump between Angelina in 1935 and the woman captured in oils. I ask if this woman is her grandmother. *Wendell's passion was landscapes, this is one of his few portraits, all were of me . . . including that one.* She nods to the wall, to the nude prone on the casting couch, hair winding across back to hips. I look at Angelina. She pats my cheek. *Yes, dear boy, there are others, many others, the rest are European and Middle Eastern, sculptors, architects, potters, men who worked in rock and so on. Have you seen Stonehenge?* I cannot answer. I look at the locket photo, at the miniature, up at Angelina. My hands rattle, the ceiling fan rings my ears like a propeller. *Come! This mystery is simple . . . and opportune.*

Angelina's hand is warm as she leads me back to the teal flower mirror. A wave of her arm, and the looking glass reflects us at age 20. *Don't we make a fine couple. Your body is 50, mine is 90. You can choose which side of the glass is real.*

I look at her lined face, at the cover girl in the mirror.

When you were two years old, Jean's mother bathed you and washed your clothes after you fell in the duck pen. She was afraid your mother would never let you come back to play. Your first girlfriend Cindy yelled SHIP in her home, a juvenile play on words. In college, the lass you lived with, Leanne, had a ménage a trois with your ex-girlfriend and her husband while you were at class. Need I go on?

I rub my forehead, damp palm trembles.

You're married. Have two adult children. If we walk through the mirror, we'll be the couple you see. I am the ultimate patron and siren of muses. I guarantee you seventy glorious years. You will become a great poet, verse will drip from your fingers like sweat from a racehorse.

I look to the floor, to the window.

I'm a very wealthy woman. We can go into space in a decade or so, that's one of your dreams. Your children—we can befriend them, you know what they like. I can insure good lives for them. Your wife will be secure and not alone. I will find her a kind companion.

Angelina waves at the mirror again. We look 20 in 2003. She wears a baby doll tee and cargo shorts, a small red nose stud, rubies above triple platinum loops on her ears; hair dreadlocks to waist.

I don't look at her image for me.

She pulls me towards the mirror. The door creeps open behind me.

Between The Devil and the Deep Blue Sea

Loose sighs at his naked
novices   dripping Sea of Salt
new souls to tutor in torture
each issued a pitchfork
forged to their palms
they will eat with it
shovel crimson embers with it
wipe their rear with it

Loose dreams he's on the Deep Blue
Sea   sways in a wicker basket
names each outline of stars
for a lover or hunting buddy
drifts against the current
up a diligent river
a young woman plucks him out
of wadding to be her pet   but

Loose will not eat red coal
his punishment   dwell amid it
skin turning ashen
tissue blind to touch
water is not forbidden
it evaporates in his stride
last he crossed the Red Sea
Moses and minions followed

Loose lusts for dead senses
it's training day every day
drilling novices
to be numb while
jabbing sizzling filleting
the raw recruits who recoil
their pitchforks dissolve
The Devil desires that deal

Ritual

Nine steps from *beys-hakisey* to yawning door
left foot first, smile in the mirror on **seven**
end with left sole curled on the marble threshold

Ten paces from threshold to bedside table
right foot first, lay eyeglasses on table on **six**
spin left heel land *hintn* and right arch on bed

Pull up sheet next quilt next comforter to chin
check *kishn*, the open case points east on **five**
fit arms to sides elbows to hips thumbs to palms

Do you count and pace in perfect alignment
trace your pleas, mark gasps of *tfile* on **four**
in harmony with kin who warded off jackboots?

Chant blessings Hebrew aloud English silent
lose a place, start over on odd try like **three**
curl west arm under *kop* face The Holy Land

Yiddish translations:
beys-hakisey—toilet (or bathroom) from Hebrew, literally "house of the seat"
hintn—tushi
kishn—pillow (or cushion)
tfile—prayer from the Hebrew tefilah or l'hitpalel, meaning "to judge oneself"
kop—head

Romeo & Juliet at Auschwitz

we wear only indigo digits
        march through white doorways
                a deaf echo as latches slam
        chlorine with a hint of vomit
families unite in the jaundice of a bulb

father mother I twine fingers
        eyes are deserts
                kiss my kup rub my cheeks
        we whisper names
seek G—d in the shade

                        in my bed
                    I dreamt of D'Vorah
                untied her white nightgown
              flannel whispered to the floor
            my seed splattered on holy sheets

                      at kheyder
                my eyes sipped D'Vorah
            her slate acted as a mirror   she
        spied my stares   smiled   cheeks ripe
        as wine   captured me in her fertile vine

a hand squeezes my shoulder
        D'vorah
                this is not my dream
        I'm limp
flush on concrete

the ceiling hisses   we chant
        wedding vows kiss Her
                bounty is boundless as the sea
        Would I were sleep and
peace so sweet to rest

Time to link
        arms with our parents
                sing the Shema   not
        climb for pockets of air
six numbers six names six candles

A recent National Geographic survey indicates that eleven percent of the young people in this country can't locate the United States on a map

three floors in this old wood house
our rooms are on the first
I can climb out my window day or night
stay in the shadows   sneak out to Shepherd Street
can always tell that road   sidewalks have lumps
Ma says they're from frost but they last all year
if I go right at the dead chestnut tree
that's Doyle Road   most times a traffic jam
horns and sirens all night   Doyle has a new walk
all black tar   hot in summer   follow it
four blocks   past Greensboro Ames Columbus
to Calvin with the boarded up mansion on the corner
some say it's haunted but I spent a night there
didn't see no ghosts but smelled a lot of pee
Calvin Road has cracks in its sidewalks
sometimes I jump 'em   other times step on 'em all
go past Hilliard Avenue and Haines Alley
come to my school   yellow brick walls
windows that don't open   playground has broke rides
next right is Macmillan   fire station as I turn
new concrete walkway 'cause of firetrucks
halfway up the block are my cement hand prints
in front of Stacy's pink house   so she'll see 'em
every time she walks to school or gets the bus
take Macmillan past Columbus Ames Greensboro
back to Shepherd   has a gas street light
next to the sign   light winks   STOP sign has no P
walk by seven three deckers   back to my window
when Ma is pissed at me she locks it then the door
I keep an old mattress and pillow under the stoop
found them one trash day

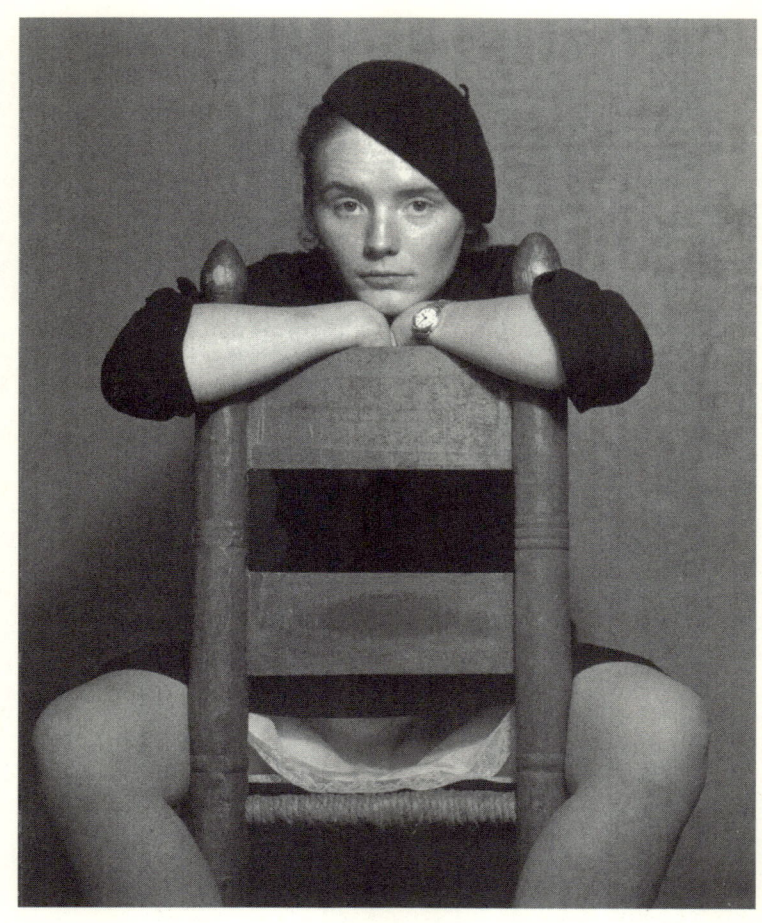

Charis Wilson, 1935
Photograph by Edward Weston

Charis

—*from an Edward Weston photograph* Charis Wilson *(1935)*

II.

sits on a chair after a day in the desert
arousing the photographer's muse
he wheels out his camera
frames low calf to above beret
while he focuses under the darkcloth
does she think of her fatigue?   reheating the pea soup?
her love of this man who lives for the well felt negative?
is she ready to grab her pen
capture him in manacles of prose
let loose the beam beneath her brow?

III.

it is five after four

Atlas and Sisyphus break for tea

Atlas jams the knob of the broom borrowed from The Witch of Endor under the moon,
wedges its bristles between the Balkans.

Sisyphus, about to crest Atlas' ribcage, claps.
The boulder bounds out of his arms, bounces off Atlas' butt, Sisyphus close behind.

Let's order badam tea from Starbucks with bagels, bistro boxes, and bananas.
You foot the bill with your Bronze card.

Sisyphus belches a sovereign's sigh,
beckons to the drive-through barista for grande cups and brown bags.

Atlas bolts bologna with a slab of brie.
My task was born by feeble believers. From earth's badlands, I bear the heavens.

There is no up in a weightless nebula, gravity's whirligig, big bang's barophobia.
Sisyphus spits a black olive pit at his boulder.

'Til your tunic busted I thought you wuz a hill.
That hogback ridge your bulbous buttocks.

Badder than rubbish, your bouquet robs breath.
Lie down, my task will cease from your crease.

Atlas and Sisyphus abandon their buffet.
Broom is parked back in parabolic orbit, shoulder pushes boulder over tibia.

Atlas bombards Sisyphus with breadcrumbs.
Sometimes an apple is just an apple, but a bitten pair can be just as bitter.

Better living through cancer

You will take each day and get through it and always
remember that each day is a success. By the way, you
look mighty cute in your radiation outfit.

ARLENE ETTA FOX EISNER (1950–2013)
IN LOVING MEMORY

And in honor & memory of loved ones lost this year to cancer
Priscilla Brown, Darlene Spector, Jan Sypek, and Kate Carlson

and Clan Webster classmates
Gina Cardamone-Raynor and William T. Eldred Jr.

for you in the battle, Stay Strong! Believe
in the power of prayer by strangers.

Agita

If I die today bury me in this purple blanket
I'd ask for the dog too curled in the crook of my arm
he isn't the one with cancer and likes you more
if you have shiva to sit he'll fill your lap
thanks for cleaning the floor when I pass out
and spill formula from the PEG tube
please hold my head as I vomit
blanket bleeds all our scents
my drink drool and food stains
in the grave totem
not for my warmth
but my nose
triggers
faith

Bitterness is like cancer. It eats upon the host. But anger is
like fire. It burns it all clean.   —Maya Angelou

framed on the wall   Julie Andrews Ozzie Osbourne Kathleen Battle
        surgeon dictates
large tumor difficult access
unknown source—maybe red dye #2? bad luck!
fourteen hour surgery
incision under right ear down to collar across and up center of throat
flap peeled back to excise cancer must prune suspicious lymph nodes
nerves will be severed   unable to lift arm above shoulder
        surgeon sips water
I can do you next week   you may wish to consult an oncologist
        glances at my wife
oh, and treasure your time together.

horns outside   The Spanish Grille Santiago Liquors Rodriguez MiniMart
Pontiac Tempest lists over a curb smoke pummels closed hood
        drivers dial cell phones behind locked doors
Toyota Celica eases behind the Tempest four boys pile out
driver points to his trunk *!Agarra las mantas y los extintores de fuego!*
two go to the Tempest lift out a grandfather and grandmother
ferry them to folding chairs in front of Family Dollar
whisper *¿Puedes respirar bien? ¿Tragaste humo?*
the rescued shake their heads
with toothy smiles the boys try *Sit, we take care of fire*
join their friends smothering the engine

oncologist introduces   Radiation-Oncologist new Surgeon Hematologist
on an exam chair I am jacked up to their eye level
biopsy slides are loaded   CAT scan fleshes my tumor on a screen
camera snakes up my nose down my throat   doctors ring around a monitor
more to the left says one my nostril tickles *a little lower—there!* chimes another
they guide me to a conference table
        oncologist comforts
do not want to overwhelm ask questions can take a break
cancer caused by HPV virus
nine weeks inductive chemotherapy
thirty-five radiation treatments
cure rate eighty percent

Dad says Grace

—For Melvin Fox on his 90th birthday

I

gathered in the whipple waiting room
we trade tales of Dad

    flashlight flush to chin flame cheeks he follows us
        wails *OOOOOOOOOOWWWWWWWWW*
        we giggle slow to be caught raised to the ceiling

   hair blown back around bald spot motoring the convertible
        brother-sister-brother bounce on back seat
        rain falls top stays down *takes Einstein to raise it*

  three generations of progeny learn to crow
        My name is Yon Yohnson, I come from Wisconsin, I work
        by the lumber mill there in the same off key cacophony

Mom stops pacing calls the nurse hears laughter in the OR asks
     What's the delay?
        nurse replies *Have to wait to stabilize his blood levels.*
        Meanwhile he's telling us joke after joke.

II

I drive Dad into Boston today is liver biopsy day
a long needle in the abdomen while the patient is awake
Dad asks to stop for coffee for Mom & me
comments on steel sky orange leaves wispy clouds
asks if I remember the foliage train into Vermont
wonders where we should eat on the ride home

III

Dad is bedridden
weighs less than homecoming from Guam
he smiles when I walk into his room
I tell him I have cancer
he asks *What can I do?*

Day One

my nurse gives me a red three ring binder
green and blue tabs mark:
       chemotherapy side effects
       radiation side effects
       health care proxy
       Bard PowerPort surgical insertion
          and bleeding
       PEG feeding tube surgical insertion
          and infections
       anesthesia
       anti-nausea drugs
       weight loss and nutrition
       diarrhea and constipation
       steroids and insomnia
       pain pills and pain patches
       wigs and scarfs
       sexual dysfunction

I carry my binder to the elevator
waiting there   a whistling man
sunken eyes   bald   no eyebrows
CANCER SUCKS button on his backpack
he grins at me and asks
"So what are you in for, kid?"

CAT Scan

in a tube   nose inches from white plastic
IV drip feels cold then like the need to pee
whirring   table trundles
magnets' clang announces each stop
pretend I'm in a spaceship
red and blue lights flash   hydraulics hum
capsule clanks   engines fire
gravity pulls me between bolsters

close my eyes

dream of that pine tree in the forlorn field
branches tent to the ground
mingle with clay
limbs canopy
the hollow like layers of lace
dry in pelting rain
I sleep on a pallet of needles
wait for a whisper to wake me

Anesthesia

the spa has a chrome soda fountain
glass case with shelves of penny candy
a rack of comic books creaks
the warped pine floor groans   crackles
I amble to the maple phone booth
rotary dial   dome light   cableless phone book
no label with directions for local or long distance
I flip my finger in forgotten circles   click-cl
ick-click   the digits to call my parents
I hear three buzzes then six then twelve then
hang up and let my fingers do the walking
Margo's number   again a dozen tones   no reply
I try Margo a second time and a third for luck
drum my fingernails against the molasses wood
kick the door below the glass   shoulder out
a few drops of rain thud against the spa's window
outside   a sudden flash of light   boom
the spa lights dim   blink   go cold   tapping
with my shoes   I feel the path back to the booth
Margo   my parents   I dial counting holes
flipping my finger to the metal bridge   no answer
Margo once more   I lean to the booth wall   sag
onto wooden slat   sit with receiver on ear
chin to chest   buzz-silence   buzz-silence . . .
the counting of heartbeats

The Alphabet of Head & Neck Cancer

Aquaphor under gauze, the latest rage in scarfs
Baclofen bucks the hiccups, shutters the eyes
Cisplaton rides the arteries' rapids, scorches skin
Diarrhea toilet art, lime snakes to yellow flakes
Educate a student nurse, be her first stomach injectee
Fungi in stir fry yum, not so much growing on the tongue
Gingiva cracks and sores, collateral damage
HPV caused the carcinoma, too late to vaccinate
Implanted port-a-cath, pin cushion to the chest
Jevity formula fills the tummy; talk while feeding, dummy!
Kids the true heroes, no complaints about their hair
Lesion on my hip turns green, scalpel drains it clean
Magic Mouthwash numbs my maw, can yawn without yells
Needles agents of terror, now butterflies
Oral cancer not oration, hoarse not hearse
PEG tube backs up from the belly, rush rinse cycle
Questionnaire as to my health, no I do not feel sick
Radiation to 'Trane's *Ascension*, techs get the treatment
Steroids puff up the profile, provide all night pep
Toothbrush a tool of torture, graze a gum gruesome
Ulcers pock the palette, a sneeze is a mallet
Volunteers offer water and snacks, swallow war veterans
White blood cell count plummets, three day hospital vaca
X-rays MRI's & scans, my innards star on the big screen
Yeast infection coats my throat, lucky I can't taste the tonic
ZPAC kills bacteria, one more pill for the cafeteria

Chemo Brain

Lost in the grocery store you've shopped in
since you pushed a cart for your Mama? Have
a cup of Peppermint Tea, the red box on the
shelf opposite your belt buckle. Leave your
pants alone, grab a couple of bags, stumble
four aisles left to the household articles,
choose a ceramic mug, #1 DAD or I'M GETTING
TOO OLD FOR THIS SHIT or I FART WHAT'S YOUR
SUPERPOWER? Next to the pharmacy is a water
dispenser with twin taps: boiling and cold.
Put the tea bags in your mug, tags over the
rim. Fill with your preference but hot must
be best because you are shivering suddenly.
Suppose shopping is a spoiled idea when you
wanderlust for two hours to fill a thirteen
item list. Perhaps you should sit down here
on the floor til your wife can pick you up.

Nitrous Oxide

the dentist   syringe in hand   bags under eyes
out the window ole Charley weaves across the street
turns my head   apologizes for the pinch of the needle
cars hit their brakes   drivers their horns
ain't nothing I tell him   yesterday while
Charley takes two steps   makes the sign of the cross
the oncologist sliced open a green lesion on my hip
takes three steps and salutes the white lines
my phone kept ringing and it was under my ass
as he crosses a yellow pair   a pickup truck swerves by him
had a choice of missing the call or bleeding my briefs
dumps a deer carcass   Charley administers last rites
waiting for the Novocain to kick in   I play drums
I hear quick steps   the dentist rips the apron from my chest
on the instrument tray with toothbrush and pick
there's a bomb threat he says   won't hurt my mouth says I

Naked in four acts

Nana, Mom circle a beach blanket
hands strip down my dripping bathing suit
a towel chafes sand from sunburnt skin
I toddle off, wander Revere Beach

peel wrestling tights, tunic, socks, jock strap
compare snips and skins in the shower
bantamweight welterweight cruiserweight
run to lockers snapping rolled towels

she hangs wrung clothes from a curtain rod
pertly rolls the duvet off pillows
piles it in three folds at bed's foot
my clothes form a puddle on the floor

oncologist selects scalpel blade
hand the nurse my johnny and Jockeys
lay on slab under surgical lights
what's a fresh slice of flesh between friends?

Hair

I

dawn, before the squamous cell carcinoma
05:15, ride the Lifecycle and shave
      rotation of the pedals
      stroke of the blade
up the neck over the chin cross the cheeks
plow widow's peak to nape, till ear to temple
      06:15, rinse razor
      apply HeadLube Glossy Lotion

II

my radiation oncologist ticks off with digits
      mouth sores
      tongue ulcers
      throat lesions
      fungi infection
      swallow obstructions
      stomach tube
      neck burns
      pain patches
he pauses and smiles, steeples his fingers
      Don't need to mention hair loss!
I clasp my palms, rejoin
      Finally a perk and you weren't going to tell me?

III

      the shower drain
    clogged again, body hair
my toes peel strands, pipe gurgles
      between my legs
    two hairless chihuahuas
      bark at the spray

IV

a beard scratches the pillow
        probe my face, whiskers!
inspect my neck, smooth over scar tissue
        canvass my cranium, baby soft filaments!
my bald spot? once an orange, now a plum!
        further perk of chemo and radiation
hair loss restoration
        not one I'd recommend

Little Bang

—my Novalis Tx radiosurgery platform

midnight blue johnny with houndstooth pattern
gray sweatpants white tube socks Rocky walking shoes
take out earring   take off eyeglasses
cue iPhone to play BeJae's *Red Cross Woman*
sit on slab   rotate rear
legs down   feet towards control booth
head between tech's palms eased onto plate
shoulders pulled up to left   back to right
the mask appears   floats in air
crown for face neck and chest to nipples
deep breath hold release again deep breath hold release
the mask goes from solid white to mesh to flesh
locks onto nose   snap from top of head
snap from left   right   left   right
shoulders and slab   head and plate   are one
room to inhale exhale   grunt answers
music on   fluorescents off
alone in sealed bunker
Little Bang hums   her arms wave
one opposite my left ear   another hovers my face
on a small screen   green and red LED's run Donkey Kong
and stop   green beam from left   off   pause
red beam   I am radioactive

Mesh Radiation Mask

—reticulum radialis larva

Dimensions: 18.5 in x 22.875 in (47 cm x 58 cm)

Description: Device covers from the crown of the skull extending
over the face and neck down to the nipples. Material is a bone
colored mesh plastic, pliable when soft rigid when hardened. Mask
is formed from a clay mold of the target area. Nose and mouth
are fabricated to permit passage of air and coughing without
body movement. Wearer can utter words without compromising
position. If nostrils itch wearer must ignore. Should the wearer
have a Port-a-Cath, a slot can be slit to allow for IV lines.

Usage: Have wearer sit on the middle of the lead slab. Rotate
legs to bottom of slab, head to the mount at the top. Pull wearer
up until crown of head is in line with slab edge. Center skull on
mount. Hover mask over wearer. Lower matching nose channel to
organ. On contact with mount, snap the rear latch followed by side
latches alternating left and right. Be certain wearer is able to speak
and breathe but is unable to move target area. After radiation
routine finishes, release the side latches then the top latch. Hold
wearer's nose while lifting mask off face.

Caution: Radiation will cause external burns, peeling, and possibly
lesions on target area. Take this into account while applying and
removing mask. Application of Aquaphor covered by gauze is
recommended between treatments.

Note: After completion of thirty-five treatments, wearer has the
option of retaining the mask. It may be kept as a memento or
reused as a life preserver.

Time bomb

loiters
saliva surfing
until the day it gnaws DNA's apple
shoots craps with other cells
snake eyes signifies malignancy

all those years of salivation
I crawl a maze of fears
        airplane crashes?
        ice propels car off bridge?
        anesthesia stops heart?
        killer lurks in dark alley?
        motorcycle lane splits?
        red meat bungs veins?
        beer drowns discipline?

after the explosion
petty fears are annulled
tomorrows will follow
        or not

I have this day to keep
        totter slower than toddler
        too swollen to swallow tongue
        words lost as soon as read
        convulsions wracking limbs
        sunshine heating my comforter
        dog curling under my arm
        son's voice soothing my confusion
        whispering wife wipes my face

Radiation Brain

Blue couch. Asleep? Awake? Nap twenty hours a day, don't know which twenty. Dream about peeing into a wastebasket at the multiplex then a flowerpot in a bathroom with a sealed toilet. Long, satisfying; splattering counters, ceilings, pants.

Still need to pee. Spot the TV. Same show playing, maybe same argument same tight end dropping a football over and over. Opposite wall, photographs ooze down, leave long trails. Sure that's the floor. Aim feet at photos. Rock to stand, land on back, bang head. No worries, no pain, but need to pee. Climb couch, wallow to bathroom. Sit. Listen. Stream.

Back to couch. Lie on other side. Sun pours in, eyelids red. Forget to turn lights out? Pillow wet? Mouth dry. Should take sweatshirt off. Must sit to do that so will bake. Who turned the TV on? Crotch cramping, need to pee again. Pull pillow off face, spy wall behind. Damn! Dog toys on wall. Coffee table legs. Carpet. Target toes towards wall. Roll. On feet and standing. Without bouncing off floor. Brilliant!

BeJae

daily, I pick euphony to fret
Little Bang's bound choreography
my neck, radiated red saddles

the ride home, like you I dream of cars
rouse to pegged tongue strung to parched mouth nut
climb stairs, arm in Ann's bridge hand on rail

on my couch, I strum a blog entry
four hours three verses two fingers
one key off garble, mended by spell check

in dark, I wait to tune in comments
your response blows morphine off my stage
a warm pickup, you call me Cupcake

Let all our vows and oaths, all the promises we make and
the obligations we incur to you, O God, between this Yom
Kippur and the next, be null and void should we, after
honest effort find ourselves unable to fulfill them. Then
may we be absolved of them.   —Gates of Repentance

forty-four years
the day of Kol Nidre

I swing and swig a gallon of water
eat a larger sandwich at lunch
add a bag of chips and brownie
greet dusk with supper's seconds
in shul, I heed the duet of cello and organ
draw my sins in sighs against stomach
confess my transgressions seven times
as the prayers repeat
I spy a baseball field in front of the bimah
miniature players pitching, running, fielding
hitting home runs to supplicants' punches of chest
teams escape to dugouts as the sermon begins
Rabbi wishes us an easy and fulfilling fast
stuffed at the end of the service
I am starving

the Rosh Hashanah marked
by the end of radiation

Rabbi visits me at home
informs me I am forbidden to fast
holding hands, we pray
in the den, no space for a baseball field
I pour formula into the stomach tube
blood pounding in my ears

since recovery
I must sip water often

for Yom Kippur
a full breakfast, skip lunch
eyes close for cello and organ
as the liturgy plays out, baseball teams emerge
I listen to singing and davening, try to join
but am bothered by bored whisperers
a teen in torn blue jeans and plaid shirt
a cantor imposing modern melodies
the new rabbi preaching metaphors
I yearn for the sermons of the old
he knew the count of my qualms, how to pitch
God dared me with cancer, watched over
three Cheerios in an orange cup taunting
singed taste buds, mouth a mass of sores
crippled throat, pocked tongue

In the fog

—for Darlene

the next chair is open
        my nurse seats you
another body in a johnny
        plugs IV pump to pic line
utters your name
        my cotton ball brain stirs
you are my cousin
        now infusion room crony

we talk shop
        you have two ports
I one
        my tumor oral
yours ovarian
        (we do not say
no babies)
        two surgeries for you
radiation for me
        I can't swallow
you vomit what you eat
        music gives you migraines
reading is möbius for me
        our view is Boston's skyline
toes heated by sunshine
        bodies draped in hot blankies
(almost makes being here
        worth the pain)

nurse brings our next round
        petite cups of pills
you chug yours
        I force mine down one by one
we compare med colors
        contrast bowel movements
you laugh
        I hiccup

(not your regular hiccups
        —industrial strength)
we are quiet
        my breath held
body spasms
        you shiver and grimace
nurse wraps you in new blankies
        changes pouches on the pole
she wears gloves apron
        chemo burns skin (Warning!)
it chugs along our veins
        I call it my battle buddy
five and a half liters of fluids
        plus a diuretic

I grab you a sandwich lemonade
        toll house cookies
for me a bottle of water
        vanilla pudding cup
we trek to the bathrooms
        rolling our twin pumps
sipping is bee stings
        but I can pee chemicals
into porcelain bubbles
        flush both systems

at your memorial I learn
        I was a comfort to you
you were to me too
        we can't exchange that memo

Arlene

the last time we speak is by phone
        I ask how you are
    the answer quickly coils on me
    how's my weight?
    can I read books? write?
    you recall hiding your Dad's candy
    he blamed it on your Mom
        I spin the tale of three brothers
    our fathers and uncle playing rummy
    sparring spades with quips
    each the alpha shark

you first battle at age twenty-eight
        ovarian cancer
    doctors offer two years
    daily, you wake smiling
    phone friends fighting the disease
        pain a pit to ramp
      pity a puddle to jump
    you win the microcellular combat

a tumor spawns on my tongue
        your call is the first
    every day an email
    every week a card
        you teach me to hunt humor
    rhumba to belch-hiccup melodies
    savor loss of plots in repeat sitcoms
        if I'm angry
    you tell me to be kind to myself

I'm born from treatment cancer free
        when I can eat solid food you celebrate
    when my stomach tube is removed you rejoice
    when I weigh the same as before you weep
        I ask about you now in your second battle
    you quip about procedures
    ask about my sons   so
    I will ask about your daughter and grandsons

when I can drive
                we meet for doughnuts
      you thinner
      me wishing to give you flesh

we pray for others in treatment

you mobilize for a third battle
                this enemy is pancreatic
      we schmooze when you can speak
      gold marks sheer ridges you scale
      bouncing to your feet after falls
      tightening your lines
                above treeline at age sixty-two
      the ropes burst

                I still talk to you
                        hear laughter

                if I feel sorry for myself
                        a chiding

                you never succumbed
                        passed us
                                your standard

Clan Webster

Some things have to be believed to be seen.

MADELINE L'ENGLE
MANY WATERS, 1986

Oh, Missouri

—for BeJae Fleming

night wraps me in missouri air
      body a beer can on steam radiator
          i breathe the mississippi
             wildrice husks
                cattail blossoms
                      lamina offerings from moss clung ferns
                i dream waves to the delta
            bob cajun fishing boats
         roust crawfish on current
     i am hungry
the river whispers gumbo . . .

Cuivre River State Park   5am   1971

grenadine dawn
through the crack in the tent
sun shafts my eyes

she lies next to me
crimson walls filter rays
burgundy bedroll rises

falls   lifts fingernails
imprudent poppies
point to damask cheeks

to trace my ruddy index
along her ruby jaw
outline her scarlet nose

unlace her claret gown   spy
the reds of her body
vermillion   auburn   flame

here in morning beams
now   orange   yellow
a kiss shatters dreams

Madeline

the night we meet we lie on your bed talking
a big black man sleeps in the bedroom chair
can of Busch Bavarian in his hand
every hour or so he startles and sips
snorts and sails back into his dream

six in the morning we crawl off the mattress
stretch the way to your kitchen
coffee   toast with honey
pick up cans and bottles   empty ashtrays
wash dishes and mugs   share a joint

that day in your basement bibbing beer
sunbeams spike the window through tree branches
smoke waves scatter dust in solar tides
The Low Spark Of High Heeled Boys spins
we are charmed by our chairs' chatter

Match of the wooden soldiers

You fork a knight with index and ring, slap the clock,
light a Lucky Strike with the last butt,
blow rings into the tale,
how you left your right middle finger in 'Nam,
stumped by a booby trap door.
You whistled at blood pulsed spray,
tied a tourniquet with teeth.
The medic looked at your eyes,
hid the morphine.

Our best girls bribed us with Budweiser and biscuits.
Did we avoid this match or was it your bait?
I babble about dodging lightning on Mount Lee's summit.
You hack and spit in the ashtray,
block your queen.
A Richter-Veresov Attack ends in another stalemate.
I hunger for stories to match yours.

You raise a pinkie, limp to the lav with spoon and lighter.
I reset the clock,
set the pieces in formation.
You return, strike a Vienna Opening.
The timer's tick eats clack of pan and pot.
I volley a Latvian Gambit.
Twelve hours, twenty-four Buds, eight tacos, two massages, twenty checks,
no mates.

Amid a Goring Gambit,
you whisper about leave in Bangkok with boot camp buddy Willie,
about the whore shared.
As she took you, a blush rashed your cheeks.
Willie howled
You white boys are sooooo uptight, 'fraid I'm gonna see sum'in' I dig?

At the sixteenth hour, Sokolsky's Opening is stalled by Slav Defense.
We slap palms above the battlefield,
agree to match in a week.
Three days later,
you lay on bathroom tiles, needle in arm, tourniquet relaxed.
I meet Willie at the cremation, shorter, thinner than expected.
We burn my chess set that night,
piss on the embers.

1971

When Allen Ginsberg visited Webster College
supplicants filled the Loretto-Hilton Theatre
the beat opened with *Howl*
heard many lines echoed
pausing for sips of water
he surveyed the suits the chic the freaks
offered the house his thermostat
a baritone *Please Master*
hippies nodded their heads
waved peace signs
he swallowed a sly smile
rumbled through *America*

> there was a VIP reception
> there was a VIP banquet
> there was a VIP apartment

> > > instead

Allen Ginsberg strolled dormitory halls
room to room he considered canvases
slid proffered poems into his pouch
kvelled over a newly fired goblet
in the kitchen he called out ingredients
assembled a macrobiotic meal
guitars sax fiddle set a meter
matched by knife to board

lotus in a circle sharing common bowls
he led chants a meditation
pulled out finger cymbals danced
shadowed by young feet
on an empty bed in someone's room
dirty sheets stained quilt patchouli
he flopped snored the night
endured cafeteria breakfast

Allen Ginsberg rode to the airport
in a car bereft of reverse and first gears
grateful the window rolled down

Mrs. Noah's Bitch

—for Jane Ellen Ibur

I had an in on this ark
Mrs. Noah raised me from a puppy
feeds me morsels from her fingers
cuddles me to her breasts for sleep

she doesn't mind I'm home for fleas,
ticks, worms, mites, unnamed parasites
they won't breed until we walk on land
I thought my job was to whelp puppies

Noah's dog is sergeant-at-fangs
his post, sever the food chain
mark limits by lifting a leg
guard his master's door at night

before the ark, I had a mate-to-be
who licked my snout, rolled in puddles
we chased in Mrs. Noah's pasture
dug dirt, he let me have the bones

now my mate-to-be rots in the flood
I imagine him paddling after me
until his paws could no longer churn
who sentences the gentle to drown?

Noah's dog will bend to mount me
he'll bite my neck, bleed my nose
pups will suckle, romp tails-a-wag
until their stud teaches them to kill

woman and bitch birth new generations
Mrs. Noah and I see foam on the sea
the best favor we offer Mother
change course, embrace the currents

Unloading reefers with Edgar

—reefers = refrigerated railroad cars, sub zero

Edgar calls out to his best friend *Hey Greek*
riding by on a double pallet jack
The Greek is a Cyclops warehouse foreman
       who never locks the toilet door
cocks his head at eagle's angle to hear
draws a bead with his glass eye to shrug NO

Edgar burps and pops me in the shoulder
Time to earn The Blowser folding money.
she is his patronne he her hosanna
       I fancy a contrary dame
on a mattress that smells like no other
catch only glimpses through tinted windshields

Edgar cracks the rail door a frozen breeze
we join siding to car with the dock plate
I strain lifting my side he hums "Taps" winks
       we lock it in place with steel pegs
pull a pallet off the heap to the plate
he grins *Watch this—here come the college boys!*

The tall boys sport buttoned designer jeans
hooded football sweatshirts basketball shoes
Edgar wears navy pants with random rips
       he is short old built like a plug
his boots are scuffed creased soles separating
brown jacket an impressive stain array

Edgar motions me north of the pallet
prods the yawning boys to the south corners
explains the task he will toss and we stack
       the boys nod I smother a laugh
he hops in the sixty four foot boxcar
wiggles loose the first 40 pound cases

Edgar grabs one in each hand flings the pair
never turns from the wall of frozen fries
I catch and set cases into the block
              tap my foot to his whistled tune
cases elude the boys slide off the pile
they scramble to spin them back into place

Edgar stops when he counts to 48
eight per layer six high closes the pallet
the boys drop a few off of the dock plate
              jump down on the track to fetch them
amid broken bottles varmint feces
slivers of creosote piddled pebbles

Edgar shouts *Hey Greek, got one just for you!*
the Cyclops runs his jack under and lifts
elevates the good eyebrow towards us
              jiggles his muzzle at the boys
shinnying up from the track now slimy
he rides off we pull-push a new pallet

Edgar hikes the potatoes like nerf balls
I follow his backbeat catch-stack catch-stack
the boys think about constructing a block
              forearms stumble on flummoxed brains
they fumble thwack a layer to my side
knock me off the plate face first to the track

Edgar grabs my parka collar in one paw
flicks me up before I smack glass ties rock
eases me on the plate clucking his tongue
              boys, you gotta be much smarter
why don't you stand back and watch us a bit
I deploy myself behind the pallet

Edgar flails cases faster than before
I capture and nestle two at a time
we polish off the pallet in seconds
              The Greek unsummoned pulls it out
in twenty minutes we've cleared the doorway
my heart is hammering undershirt drenched

Edgar rubs his palms smiles savagely
Coffee break. *Be back in ten primed to work.*
The Greek arrives with carafe and sinkers
          sugared cake filled with red jelly
Thanks Greek, The Blowser don't allow no sweets.
Afraid I might lose my teeth and not bite!

Niagara Falls, 1972

engine squeals, fan belt slaps severing all ties
    the gas pedal becomes a foot rest
in fading twilight, two pairs of feet track
    thunderclaps drown their steps
they sprint through puddles giggling and shivering
    register as man and wife in the motel shack

their cabin has one twin bed
    she hangs wet blouse and jeans—*I'll shower first if that's ok*
he dangles wet t-shirt and cutoffs next to hers

she emerges wearing a white towel
    drapes it over the headboard
        raises the patchwork quilt
            folds back the sheets
                arranges the pillows
                    slips into bed

he retreats into the bathroom
slides off underwear
lets hot stream douse hair
wraps towel round waist
leans on tub patting forehead cheeks chin . . .
opens door flips towel on dresser
jumps under covers

she smiles—
    Are you ok?
      You look nervous.

he met her, a college ride board refugee, at breakfast sixteen hours ago; her mother sat opposite pulling on the straps of a pale gingham dress, long blonde hair unbound, garden flower above left ear—*Thank you for taking our daughter*—her father patted his back, shook hands nodding slowly, kissed his child on the cheek, opened the car door, turned away

strangers in bucket seats, she told jokes, sewed a loose button on
his shirt, made sandwiches on french bread—tomatoes, roasted
peppers, fresh cilantro—smiled whenever he looked, laughed
nervously at the New York state line

she lies on her side, faces the wall, switches off the lamp
he stares at the ceiling, holds breath, hears the current of her sighs
break on white pillowcase

he could brush the hair off her shoulder
      trace the shape of her arm
           stroke the course of her spine
               to her hip
                    across her thigh
                         drift along belly—her rounded belly

tomorrow feet in cold stirrups

he sleeps on his back, hands on stomach

in the morning, the motel manager asks *How's your wife?*
snaps a shot of the couple, brunette and blonde in greyscale,
next to a highway sign
    "Niagara Falls 18 mi"

Joan Ellis, rest peacefully

Where is she?
Lying in blood under Puerto Rican sky

Joan bounces cross the dorm floor, hair mushrooms
You know, it's always good to have a couple of men ...
                    and a few women
snap! the tab pops off a beer
                    always a few women

Where is she?

Bobby's boot doubles the beat of the bass
Joan tickles his thigh
                    you uptight to get high?
                    ... let's go upstairs to my room

Where is she?

Homecoming '71
                    student faculty flag football
                    black hash   Pabst Blue Ribbon
                    loss of down for spilling
Professor Norm, former Spartan safety
                    blindsides sophomore Roberta
                    breaks her fibula
                    as she wails, he spins and strolls away
Joan darts over grass,
                    crackblocks the man twice her weight
                    pins his neck with her knee
                    spits blood in his face
                    Don't fuck with my sister

Where is she?

the Mustang cruises I-40 east
    Joan's left hand caresses my shoulder
    cigarette balances in the right
    bare foot hangs out the window
we, the sole volunteers at the school for pregnant girls
    guard and barb wire fence
    Kentucky Fried Chicken served through bullet proof glass

Where is she?

Joan leans the mic stand like Elvis in Memphis
her Baez cheeks belt sweet Aretha soul
pas de chat, she snatches her sax
  slides the reed in and out of her mouth
pacing the stage, she
    moans Bird
    screams 'Trane on fire
    a banshee in the dark

Where is she?

Lying silent under Puerto Rican sky,
she and her lover, hot blood dead heat

Einstein Gothic

Albert actions the wicker rocker, sips Asbach from a mason jar, wipes the rim on his overalls. He drags on a Bugler's butt, flicks it, flattens ash and flame with his heel. I stare into the rafters of the farmhouse porch, at a rowboat and oars.

My garden is goodt this year. See the tomatoes, cherry and burpless? Little globes, each red and green. Like Mars, maybe. This year, I planted finger cucumbers. My pickles will draw sweat to your temples. Cleanse the brain, never mind the bowel!

Albert snatches his .257 Weatherby. Manure and body odor ride the barrel's breeze. An equal reaction—rifle to shoulder, a little bang exhaled; 200 yards upwind, a rabbit's head divides. *Ya, flat trajectory, 87 grains at 3900 fps.*

I grab a burlap bag, Albert a pruning hook and gutting knife. *Got him before he stole a tomato. We will give him to Cook. Unlike you and me, she eats flesh.*

On the porch, Albert rolls a cigarette, strikes a stick match on his zipper. *The elimination of varmints. A quandary, no?*

Instead

—for Sister Mary Mangan, S.L., former Vogue model

For this I forsake Massachusetts for Missouri.

For this I trade *Land of Little Big Hills* for *Land of the People with Dugout Canoes.*

For this I transition from an all boys prep school to an all girls Catholic college just converted to coed colony.

For this I fly 1200 miles for $35 with a student discount on an Allegheny Airlines flight from Boston to Baltimore to Pittsburgh to Indianapolis to Columbus to St. Louis but the stewardesses let me carry on my guitar as long as I take requests and I sit next to Rita Coolidge for a leg and we both pretend I don't know who she is.

For this I live in a dorm with a roommate who also takes comfort in clutter.

For this I endure the distraught look on the director of housing's face when she tours our floor.

For this I sweat high stakes poker—loser does the laundry.

For this I jam "Back in the U.S.S.R." and "When You Dance I Can Really Love" until 3:00 am when I should cram course work.

For this I go to the turret and coffee up to stay awake in class and speak nimbly.

For this I research and write a term paper on Legislative Lobbying in four hours.

For this I chant Torah in Zady's trope so the Sisters can hear its melody and meter.

For this I coordinate a field trip to the State Capitol even though I sleep both ways on the bus.

For this I collect my corrected term paper covered with copious red remarks, most of which are complimentary.

For this I am summoned to your office to be serenely counseled that I am wasting my potential, my parents' money, and letting down my peers (who frankly are just as reckless at night).

For this I'd rather you scold me for hours.

Taxi Dancer (July 1975)

Club Muddy Waters is windowless, no a/c
two-bit bottled beer bought from a vending machine
musicians' sweaty towels dangle through belt loops

I am the pale boy sporting a biscuit beanie
she is the tan blonde brandishing the white Stetson
my crown fits under her chin like two puzzle pieces

she clutches my hand, spirals us out on the floor
leads the dance, I spin under the crook of her arm
the crush opens a swath of ample elbow room

the guitar segues from *I'm Free* into *Something*
her right palm pushes my damp shirt, rings roll my spine
left arm engulfs my shoulders, adducts head to chest

a sultry cheek caresses my stifling braincase
I see the white of her blouse, blurred fringe of dancers
she guides locomotion in time with the bass drum

thump of her heart fills one ear, Beatles the other
my cheek is clenched in her cleavage, fluids compound
a fragrance of musk, mango, maybe ambergris

underpinning the sweetness drifts a salty tang
my nose shadows the acrid scent, drawing deeply
room fades, music dims, the nub bundled in nostrils

song ceases, stocky hand presses my shoulder
I look up at a smiling man offering beer
he is as taller than the blonde than she to me

"Thanks for taking care of my girl, little buddy!"
she gives me a squeeze and a peck on the forehead
I grin, stroll to stumble on a stepper my size

Mara Blonde Punk

—from a Mark William Rabiner photograph

Mara Mother smells sweet smoke on her daughter
   Debbie readies to stay out past dawn
   she parts bleached hair, braids purple rapids
rotates brow rings, diamond stud a nostril crown

Debbie lights a cigarette, blows halos in mother's face
   Mara grips chair arms, a nail snaps
   sunlight rainbows off daughter's jewel to the photo
young Mara *that* night, the year Debbie was born

> Mara Blonde Punk prances under
> whirling lights, swaps partners with
> rhythm. Razor blade about her neck is
> spotted white. Mohawk boy fits like a
> glove, his whispered invitation singes
> her neck. Stumble up stairs, roll onto
> a roof bathed in early morning light.
> Sun rises and falls with Mohawk
> boy's eraser of black hair; his sweat
> invades her face, pulls away, returns.
> Stones scrape her buttocks, embed
> grains; purple bruises sprout on her
> shoulders from a metal strut's spars.

Mara Mother rummages a night table drawer
   tears off a strip of multi-colored packets
   with a wave and a snap, packs Debbie's purse
Debbie glares in the frame at Mara Blonde Punk

Hippie

Xavier runs through a hollow ringed by ridges
and VC   bullets whiz by *like a war movie*
his company is assaulting the enemy's tunnels
he carries an M5 medical bag   no M16

the valley is flooded from rice paddies' overflow
a cry of MEDIC cuts through explosions
he races through smoke and riddled water
to a buddy with blood spurting from a thigh

he holds the leg above water as blood bubbles
applies a Combat-Application-Tourniquet
his helmet flips off   right eye implodes
blood and shrapnel pocket his face

he puts a compress on his dead eye
one left blurs   pulls the leg back out of water
applies a bandage to the bullet hole
shoulders his patient to the Dust Off

Huey flies low fast   nurse stitches cornea
at the airport back in The World
a boy clacks a Newton's Cradle
Xavier hits the ground and rolls

Keeping time
for my history

The bottoms of my shoes
are clean
from walking in the rain.

JACK KEROUAC, *AMERICAN HAIKU*, 1959

Between three men, one woman, and a dog

—for Ann

Four for Friday dinner in my digs. Hoff—m'buddy since we wuz in diapers. Breed—engineer, peacock, choral baritone. You—Breed's med school cadaver partner, peasant blouse.

Jason Dog greets his humans, inspects bags, sniffs shoes for clues. Gives You an extra wag for lunchtime walks while I work.

Yesterday we ate at The Driftwood. Prime rib special, draft 'Gansetts. Our knives carved bloody meat, teeth chewed as Hoff & Breed depicted morning surgeries, contrasting arc & span of propelled body fluids, aromas from sundry organs. I heard a wail over my shoulder. Our waiter, face pale, wavered, fainted.

I open tonight's first bottle of Mateus, compose a toast to our brave server. Breed snorts, deglazes six garlic cloves, step one for concocting his sauces.

Hoff tosses a marrow bone to Jason, recalls the road trip to Green Bay. Humans slept heads lower than feet. Jason nudged us, groaned, slept nose uphill. Two in the morning, we woke vomiting. Jason shook his head at stupid humans. Even a puppy knows which way is up!

You haven't heard this tale of dog & men, start laughing with mouth full. Wine spurts out your nose in twin streams. We convulse hee-hawing, pawing the rug. Jason looks human to human, whines, barks crescendos, runs in circles, sniffs the air, sneezes. What broke his people?

Hoff uncorks bottle number two. There are no musical chairs or sneaking an arm around shoulders or batting eyelashes at a flirty jest. You & I rise to wash the pans, kiss our first kiss. Not like friends kiss—nostrils flared; oblivious to dropped jaws, shrugs, murmurs, an ignored bone. Jason Dog brushes our legs. *Silly humans, it took you this long?*

The Devil talks to his teenage son and gets raked over the coals

Shut the damned door behind you and take off those wingtip shoes! What have you done to your hooves? Hold them up. Higher! I want to see your red soles. Why did you bleach your hair white, why cover your horns? Are you trying to torture me? And your tail, your glorious tail, are you using your tail for a belt? With the fork for a buckle?

I don't mind rebellion, hell I invented rebellion. Hold my eyes, don't look up. By the time I was your age, I'd lost track of the souls I'd collected. You haven't bought one soul since your mother turned on me.

Your mother . . . She was the only survivor of Noah's flood. Stole the raft her sisters built, split their skulls with a staff. Deep-fried Noah's dove for dinner the night we conceived you.

I gave you a simple task yesterday. Occupy Sarah while Abraham and Isaac were away. Not snare her soul, just make small talk, flash that toothy grin, share some bread. Instead, Sarah asks about your kin, you sob, she strokes your hair, buries you in her bosom. Ten minutes later, you're pulling Abraham's knife away from Isaac's throat and sacrificing my stud ram to you-know-who.

Do you have any idea what you did? Do you know how long I worked to set that up? People will fill parchment for ages, debate the why, and guess-who will get the credit. What were you thinking?

Well, Loose Junior, quisling Loose Junior, will you say anything at all? Or do you have The Devil to pay?

TUNIS

When I stepped on African soil, I waited for my toes to burn . . .

The detour our guide chose—

Before Sidi Bou Said, white walls blue shutters gray cobblestone alleys
Before the Phoenician field of stones, each blessing a first born sacrificed to Baal
Before Hannibal's Carthage, buried by Byzantine brick and Roman marble
Before Augustus' Baths, Corinthian columns glaring like hawks at rows of catapult balls
Before the Palace of Bardo's mosaics, ancient sandstone veins

The detour passed by . . .

The United States Second World War Cemetery of North Africa
two thousand seven hundred markers in parade formation
my father's classmates
grass greener than any golf course
I yearn to walk with my sons down the rows
leave pebbles on each Cross and Star of David
let the blood beneath our soles join us to this land

In the Nick of Time

The next generation's Dylan opens with "The House of the Rising Sun"
quips he's the original, dips guitar swaying acolytes like grain to the wind

my nineteen year old son and I drove three and half hours through hail,
sunshine etched windshield, mountain blizzard curtain, and black ice

to hear this voice in this college gym . . .

The Troubadour salutes Richie Valens Jimi Hendrix The Beatles Kurt Cobain
cues cut through patchoulie, stale smoke, and the snowflake musk lovers splash

bumper sticker shirts, thin arms, hair short to skull shimmering to shoulders
knowing looks lock couples in hip improbable orbits

a girl's smile stretches farther, just when I think it will crack
blonde shag syncopates, turquoise eye winks to scoop my glance

fingers dancing chords on belt remind me of Janie's hand
sliding like plug to guitar in the side pocket of my jeans

eight gallon head in ten gallon hat, Janie's mouth drew lines cross my neck
I traversed her waist as Eric Burden crooned "The House of the Rising Sun"

our bodies filled crevices with falling rock sinew tree line curls
her soles on my shoes,

Janie splashed that smile stretched the corner of her lips to a wink
dashed tongue in ear dotting the i of that promise

I'll be back before you know it . . .

and drove her car toward Boulder off a cliff switchback
What was her final thought, did she worry her parents would be sad?

after The Troubadour's third encore, I spy the girl's smile stretching ever wider
return a turquoise wink with a grin and gray wink only she can understand

After all, it's been thirty years.

As the twig is bent, so grows the tree

—school motto

our grammar school honored someone named Flagg
no one read the cornerstone set in the shade
of the tree whose grass island split the driveway
our height was measured by leaping for branches
when we caught one, planted feet on trunk
the principal would slap our bottoms with a book
then nod unsmiling while we boarded the bus
our rote apology, "Good night, Miss White"

Amy & I shared a desk when Goldfinger was the rage
her parents forbade her from seeing the film
during class she nudged knees and grilled me
about Sean Connery's chest, what the starlets wore
(or didn't wear with whispers even quieter)
teacher gave us the glare and penalty penning
during recess we snuck behind the tree
I sated her with features of love scenes
she kissed me, asked if that's how Pussy did it

before the Pledge of Allegiance
Miss Anderson started class with a bible passage
most students were Jews who read in monotone
the assigned selection, always "Christ The Lord"
we sang Christmas carols, decorated the tree
and stayed after school still hungry
making up her tests scheduled for Yom Kippur

we scoured street and sidewalk for ciggie stubs
hid behind the tree with matches before the bell
ran coughing to the windowless side wall
joined the Butts Up game, elbowed for next throw
spat when teacher wasn't looking
split a Snickers before going inside

graduation was celebrated with faux diplomas
hot dogs, hamburgers, ice cream and pop
high school boys with sideburns plugged in
we danced to *Don't Let The Sun Catch You Crying*
Steve and Ellen were caught making out
banned from the class photo round the tree
shamed in front of parents, heroes to us

Yussel

Yus laughs at the compliment,
How do you paint a perfect line?
He cuts two strips of masking tape.
Fingers press the first on canvas,
compass aligns the second.
Brush gathers paint from palette,
fills the valley with umber river.

Yus studied in a B-24 Liberator.
Guzzled Coca Cola past flak
until eye aligned bombsight
traced a row of crackling plumes.
Messerschmitts fired tracers,
he pissed in the pop bottle,
hurled it steaming at Nazi gunners.

Yus peels the parallel masks.
Arms reach to the sky,
a bloodline divides the canvas.
He drapes sheet over easel,
winks good night,
climbs the loft ladder.
By his bed, empty Coke bottle.

Yussel's stool

inside, the B-24 is a crate
        can fist a hole through the fuselage
I twist and bend, navigate the catwalk
        tail through bomb bay to cockpit
pilots' pedals are worn, yoke chipped

outside, I hover around the front port
        angle my head, shade my eyes
I hear laughter, a man Yussel's age
        Mighty Eighth flight jacket
self-propelled wheelchair

he asks *What are you looking at, boy?*
        reply *I want to see where my uncle sat,*
dropped bombs on Nazis for 54 missions.
        he nods *Son, see the nose wheel?*
Put your back against it, reach up, climb.

I pull into the aircraft, eyes adapt to murk
        50 cal perch, pine ammunition boxes
greenhouse windows, Norden bombsight
        bombardier's stool
no way out

Yussel never dwells on flack and bullets
        Why jump out of a perfectly good airplane?
It was cold up there. There was no john.
        Shots of whiskey when we landed,
the beer at the base was balmy.

Kinder, 1960

An angel has walked among us and his name is (Rabbi) Baruch Goldstein.
—Rabbi Seth L. Bernstein, Rosh Hanshana 5760 (2000) sermon

attic classroom   kinnd draws shades
cheeks pinched   slapped with palm
grey teacher
ash bags tied by crows' feet
raps pointer on desk to silence kinder
black & white newsreels flash on cracked screen
carts filled with freight
naked children
arms hang   odd angles

kinder led single file to windowless basement
balding rabbi   black cloth kipah
waits at doorpost   rubs each kup
whispers each name
rabbi gathers flock in circle
leads berachot over
apple juice   honey cake
smiles to correct   laughs at a spill
he holds a palm out   kinder quiet
white sleeve rolls up
blue numbers
pale flesh

Life Threatening

Standing, Ann drains saline on
an eight inch gorged incision
pubic hair strains brine to
a washcloth cupped
by my hands.

2.

Don dropped that doe with
a single thirty ought six round
hit her where spine joins neck
a red stain on hide, drops of blood
curling from nose on to pine needles.
He gutted her belly—one gentle swipe
then reached in and yanked out miracles
not diagrams in the biology book, steaming
musky life. I touched the doe. She lurched.
Just spasms Don said. He handed me the heart.

3.

I ease Ann into bed. The sun caroms
from crucifix to corneas. I cover
my face with forearm, turn,
stare out the window.

4.

Crazy Charley crosses the street.
He takes three steps, stops, signs
Father Son Holy Ghost. Charley
never falters. Three steps and Trinity,
lips move, silent. Drivers jab horns,
curse, wave fists. Charley doesn't look their way.
If everyone crossed streets as he, The Messiah would come.

5.

The Ostomy Nurse removes the bag. Colon is a dark inverted nipple. I can't breathe.
It's not the gas and shit. It's this piece of Ann hidden for twenty five years.
The volcano that burst and filled Ann's abdomen so full the doctor
heard silence through the stethoscope. It winks, whispers:

believe in the purity of prayer for strangers
forget what good time you make
hold your heart in your hands
catch each drop of water
as the first

To Adam on a Utah mountainside where Navajo spirits
weave his belief that Zady is one of the righteous men
who keep this world from being destroyed

First time I recognize your eyes,
             the same eyes peering from the mirror as my link shifts in the chain,
you're on stage in *Fiddler On The Roof* wearing your aunt's vest
                                    your cousin's cap and hand-
me-down wool pants.
                    Arms to the sky in a *Why me, Lord* gesture
                  you canvas the congregation
           hazel eyes eastern European almonds, slightly off kilter

like Zady's eyes in a two room shetl shack watching feet pad the dirt floor.
        Teenagers disappear, harvested for Cossacks' trench fodder.
    Zady's father Abraham sends him on a horse (cavalry bear swords, are well fed.)
When horse and man are split, Zady slips by the guards,
                            dodges bullets.
          He travels by night, works by day,
until his eyes hold a ticket to America.

            I, the age you are now, stare
            at the picture of Abraham:
        lips pursed, our eyes, red beard
    (Zady cried when he saw your toddler hair *like my father's!*)
    My eyes dodge to my draft card, Zady's cringe at the front page photo
my fist in the air *Hell no we won't go* feet on the World War I monument podium.
    (If only Zady could see your beard, like the Tzadeeks in the old country.)

You feel different, as did I,
           Zady,
           Abraham.

                              Stubborn Ashkenazic stock
                                  hair bled with passion.
                  You fight your battle alone.
           There is no one to flee but yourself.
                                    Look in the mirror,
                      swing the chain until it rattles in place,
not like a saber,
    but pebbles in a shaman's gourd calling sacred ancestors to circle the campfire.

The Day I Was Conceived

May 2 1952   a Friday
Dad works late at the fish market
fries haddock clams scallops potatoes
wraps up salmon sole   steamers in a basket

Friday begins Shabbos
my siblings   with Nana & Zady
sister lights the candles
brother walks to shul

Dad strips his work clothes off in the foyer
puts them in the sealed metal hamper
Mom hands him a bathrobe
follows to the shower

they have dinner   maybe a drink
"Wheel of Fortune"   Kay Starr's #1 song
on the radio   Dad switches
to the ball game   Browns at Red Sox

4,106 fans flock Fenway Park   cheer
Dom DiMaggio Jimmy Piersall Vern Stephens
Walt Dropo is the star   3 hits 6 rbi's
three run homer   Sox win 13–6

a Brown's pinch hitter   Darrell Johnson
flies out to left field in the 7th   later
manages the Sox for 3 years   takes on
The Big Red Machine   '75 World Series

after the game   Dad listens to the news
blind St. Matrona   Blessed Elder of Moscow
departs this world   predicts her own death
three days in advance   sees all supplicants

De Havilland Comet G-ALYP   first passenger jet
flight   London to Johannesburg   36 travelers
two years later G-ALYP crashes off the island
of Elba   kills everyone on board   another first

in nine months   I am born by c-section
Mom chooses Groundhog Day but forgets the date
the woman I fall in love with and marry
is conceived in the quiet after my first cries

Directions

climb the mahogany staircase
polished rail in hand
make a 180 degree turn down the hall   to
a six panel door with a skeleton key lock
turn the knob   open the door   come on in
stretch your grownup arms   touch both walls
along the length of the right is a convertible sofa
  converted
white pillowcase   full length brown comforter
  triple folded at the foot
if as a child you rolled off the sofa-bed   before
  one revolution   you bumped the bureau
it was your mother's and will be your son's
three drawers for clothing
one for objects not to be displayed

opposite the door is a single window overlooking
  a brick walk and a street
in front of the window   where sitting is not allowed
  but always practiced
a small radiator covered by an aquamarine cabinet
there is a single drawer just long enough for a ruler
pull the handle side to side
slide the drawer out slowly

behold the trove of a decade:
  smooth rocks from each creek in walking distance
  dried peach and plum pits
  skunk skulls
  dead hornets
  prism and star chart
  four sticks   etched and notched
  KA-BAR in leather case with Japanese waterstone
  Eddie Bressoud lapel pin
  books of Marlboro Man matches
  magnifying glass
  Nana's last tichel
    white cotton
    embroidered sapphire flowers
    tassels
    fragrance of hair

Daycare in the 1950s

I.

Maxi The Taxi honks his horn
Nana sits up front with Max
backseat is mine to use as a trampoline or
I can lay on the shelf over the trunk
Nana holds a magic bag between her ankles
Max and I call out *COOKIES*
     warm toll house appear
we cry *CORNED BEEF SANDWICH ON RYE WITH MUSTARD*
     half a sandwich is slipped into our hands
Nu says Nana. *Do you want cherry or cream soda?*

II.

Max drops us at Tanta Zara's
she sits on her porch in the green rocker
Nana cradles me on Tanta's lap
     I am still in her bird arms
we rock, she whispers
     you have my husband's name, Rueven Hershel
     kisses wet my peak and each cheek
Max turns in the driveway
     Tanta slips a shiny dime in my hand
we ride to visit Aunt Helen and Uncle Benchke

III.

Aunt Helen unhinges a closet
carts out the cardboard box
Cousin Roger's toys
Roger dead of lupus at fourteen

I rut through wrought iron figures
     Minuteman missing arms
     Wild Bill Hickok from waist up
     Lancelot with a sword stump
     three legged Trigger
     Supergirl no ponytail or cape

I construct a fort from
        orphaned Mille Bornes cards
        amputated Lincoln logs
        furrowed wooden blocks
        train tracks missing ties
        erector set pieces bent to V's

Rolled marbles signal an invasion

The boy scout knife inscribed
        Roger guards the gate
        deployed blades and tools
        spin to divert missiles
        away from picture frames
        far away from Aunt Helen

                    IV.

Uncle Benchke yanks me up
        out the house
we don't speak
        wade into the backyard
he settles us at
        the silver dollar trees
selects a leaf
        sets it on my palm
        seals my fist
commands *Mahk ah vish*
        I do
        eyes shut

                    V.

in Maxi The Taxi
        Nana passes me a peppermint
        pinches my cheek
Nu, Roger and Benchke planted those trees.

The Fifth Floor

the entrance to the fifth floor
is guarded by a red button
high on the wall
read the sign
press the button pull the handle
a hum as the door opens

primitive art work tiles the walls
bright clumsy designs in childlike hand
the tables are covered with large stuffed dolls
stained satin pillows
toys with large beads to wind over wires
a man with glazed eyes sings cowboy songs
melodic voice dancing over a wide range
his companion mutters random syllables

Aunt Helen sits in a recliner against a table
as i speak, lips on ear
she feels her stump without expression

for months her missing knee leg and foot
have daily caused mysterious anguish
a discovery lost in scattered dreams
gangrene has renewed its assault
morphine pump a dull nightstick
she rocks and fidgets with her clothing
plays with her tube feels the stump again
rubs her hands looks down into her lap

i tell her family stories shout familiar names
stroke her arm caress her cheek
she continues the ritual in silence
the antibiotics have been stopped

at Zady's shiva
whenever the Kaddish was chanted
not just the Mourner's Kaddish
but the Reader's Kaddish or the Chazi Kaddish
Helen would pipe in loudly and hold each word
then trumpet AMEN in a big high voice

linking her fingers with mine
i chant the Shema
the words she would wish to whisper
the declaration the rites the gathering
then repeat the watchwords of faith
Shema Yisrael Adonai Eloheinu Adonai Echad!
Hear O Israel The Lord Our G—d The Lord Is One!
the last breaths martyrs utter
looking through the eyes of tormenters

the exit from the fifth floor
is guarded by a number pad
high on the wall
memorize the code
touch the four digits
a solid click as the door opens

when i return home
my first task is to wash my hands
that's what we do
when we leave cemeteries

Talmud, standing, facing Teacher

—for Bob Zinn (1950–2003)

If I am not for myself, who will be for me? But if I am only for myself, what am I?
                                                           —Hillel, "Pirkei Avot"

july 1990

that thunderstorm in Massachusetts   red pushpin on the weather map marking our tent
you volunteer to be the human pole   poke the pregnant tarp's bellybutton   its water
breaks   you leap and spit *oh shit*

the only time i ever hear you curse   i laugh till my nose bleeds

5 am, we slump the campground path   you shake knotted hair, gather the four corners,
scratch bristle, unpack half a smile, crack *what are we doing here?*

october 2002

surgeons plumb blue and red pipes into your neck   blood is laundered, comes back
bleached   you pose questions about my work   the economy   our sons & college
my poems   how fund raising will go at shul with the president tethered to bed   we
daven Maariv facing east

may 2003

the rabbi sits at your side   are there prayers to chant?   final requests?   *volunteers!*
you reply   *volunteers?* he asks   who from shul should receive awards, whose names
etched in plaques

3 am, sister holds right hand, wife the left, sons in chairs   your breathing, Teruah all
day, pauses   four short breaths, Shevarim, no Tekiah Gedolah

we cover your casket, overflow the crypt   i squeeze a handful of soil, stand at grave's
edge   *Adonai natan v'Adonai lakach, y'he shem Adonai m'vorach*   soil drips from my
fingers, rain drums the tarp